Weird Animal Diets
Soil-Eating Animals
by Teresa Klepinger

FOCUS READERS®

BEACON

www.focusreaders.com

Focus Readers is distributed by North Star Editions:
sales@northstareditions.com | 888-417-0195

Produced for Focus Readers by Red Line Editorial.

Photographs ©: Shutterstock Images, cover, 1, 4, 7, 8, 12, 14–15, 16, 21, 22, 24, 27; iStockphoto, 11, 29; Steve Gschmeissner/Science Source, 19

Library of Congress Cataloging-in-Publication Data
Names: Klepinger, Teresa, author.
Title: Soil-eating animals / by Teresa Klepinger.
Description: Lake Elmo, MN : Focus Readers, [2022] | Series: Weird animal diets | Includes index. | Audience: Grades 2-3
Identifiers: LCCN 2021034103 (print) | LCCN 2021034104 (ebook) | ISBN 9781637390559 (hardcover) | ISBN 9781637391099 (paperback) | ISBN 9781637391631 (ebook) | ISBN 9781637392133 (pdf)
Subjects: LCSH: Animals--Food--Juvenile literature. | Dust ingestion by animals--Juvenile literature. | Animal behavior--Juvenile literature.
Classification: LCC QL756.5 .K54 2022 (print) | LCC QL756.5 (ebook) | DDC 591.5--dc23
LC record available at https://lccn.loc.gov/2021034103
LC ebook record available at https://lccn.loc.gov/2021034104

Printed in the United States of America
Mankato, MN
012022

About the Author

Teresa Klepinger loves to learn about the amazing world we live in. Writing about it for kids makes it even more fun. She also enjoys helping kids write their own stories. She lives in Oregon with her family and a dog. She doesn't plan on eating soil anytime soon.

Table of Contents

CHAPTER 1

Garden Feast 5

CHAPTER 2

Getting Rid of Toxins 9

ANIMAL SPOTLIGHT

Chickens 14

CHAPTER 3

Helping an Upset Stomach 17

CHAPTER 4

Finding Minerals 23

Focus on Soil-Eating Animals • 28
Glossary • 30
To Learn More • 31
Index • 32

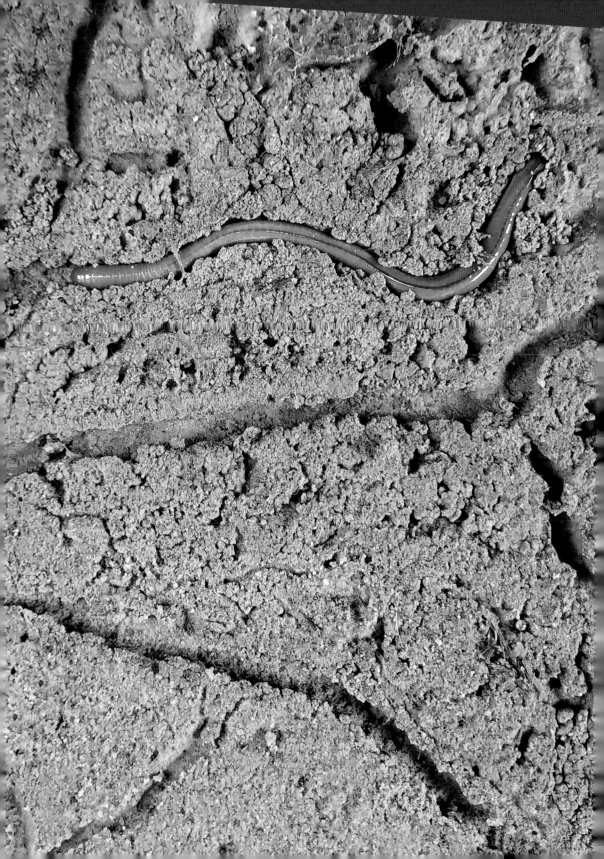

Garden Feast

An earthworm crawls underground. It eats the soil in front of it. As it eats, the worm makes a tunnel. The worm **digests** dead plants and bacteria in the soil. Then the worm poops.

 Earthworm tunnels make room for air underground.

Earthworms are important for soil **ecosystems**. By eating and pooping, worms move soil around. Their poop has **nutrients** that plants need. Their tunnels help the soil hold more air and water. Better soil helps plant roots grow and spread.

Did You Know?

Most earthworms are just a few inches long. But the longest can grow to 14 inches (36 cm).

 Bits of worm poop are called casts.

Earthworms are not the only animals that eat soil. Soil is a part of many animals' diets. Eating soil helps animals in different ways.

Chapter 2

Getting Rid of Toxins

Many plants have **toxins** in them. Plants produce these toxins to keep animals from eating them. But some animals eat the plants anyway. Toxins can cause these animals to become very weak.

 Many raw plants have toxins. People cook the plants at high temperatures to make them safe to eat.

They can make the animals throw up. So, some animals eat soil to get rid of the toxins.

For example, monkeys and some bats eat fruit, seeds, and leaves. These plant parts have some toxins in them. Too many toxins would be dangerous for the animals.

So, the animals **adapted**. They added soil to their diets. The soil has clay in it. The clay binds the toxins inside the animals' bodies. It keeps the toxins from getting into

> Clay is a soft soil made of very small particles. It is formed as rocks wear down over time.

the animals' blood. As a result, the animals don't get sick. The toxins pass safely out of the animals when they poop.

 Mold can grow when hay gets damp. So, farmers try to feed cows fresh hay.

As another example, dairy cows eat hay. Sometimes the hay has fungi in it. Fungi include mold and mushrooms. Some are poisonous to cows. So, farmers put clay in the cows' food. The fungi stick to the clay. Then the cows can poop the fungi out.

One way animals get rid of poison is by throwing up. But rats can't throw up. So, rats eat clay when they are poisoned. The poison sticks to the clay. Eating clay can help rats get better.

Did You Know?

Dairy farmers feed clay to cows for another reason. It makes the cows' milk less toxic.

Chickens

Chickens eat plants, seeds, and insects. But chickens don't have teeth. This means they can't chew their food. Instead, chickens eat tiny bits of rock called grit.

The grit and the food go into a chicken's gizzard. The gizzard is part of the bird's stomach. It is very strong. The gizzard crushes the food and grit together. The grit breaks the food into smaller pieces. In this way, the grit acts like teeth. It grinds the food. Then the food leaves the gizzard. The grit stays. Over time, it gets worn down. When it's small enough, it passes out of the chicken.

Grit can be large, rough bits of dirt.

Chapter 3

Helping an Upset Stomach

One sign of a hurt stomach is runny poop. Another word for it is diarrhea. This illness can make animals lose water. Animal bodies need water to work right. Without water, animals can get very sick.

 Like people, animals need water to live.

Some animals eat clay to help with diarrhea. These animals include chimpanzees, gorillas, and monkeys. The clay keeps them from losing too much water. It helps them stay healthy.

Eating clay can protect animals in another way. The stomach is lined with **mucus**. The mucus works like a wall. It protects the inside of the stomach. But some foods are **acidic**. They can burn through the mucus. This causes stomach pain.

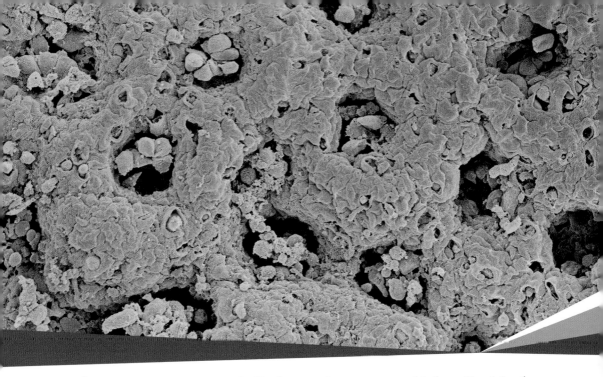

 The stomach lining releases particles that help break down food.

Eating clay can thicken the mucus. It protects the stomach. It keeps the stomach from hurting.

Some people use clay, too. They might eat food with germs in it. That can make their stomachs hurt.

To feel better, the people eat clay. The germs stick to the clay. They do not stay in the people's bodies. Instead, the people poop them out.

People have eaten certain soils for thousands of years. But eating soil can be dangerous. There are harmful bacteria in soil. There may

Did You Know?

Kaolin is a kind of clay. Scientists made a medicine out of it. It helped with stomach pain.

Some farmers spray chemicals on their plants. The chemicals may spread when it rains.

also be harmful chemicals. These things can make people very sick. People should only eat soil that is specially cleaned for eating.

Chapter 4

Finding Minerals

Many animals eat soil for the **minerals** in it. Minerals such as **calcium** help animal bodies work properly. Meat-eating animals get these minerals in their food. But not all plants have these minerals.

 Eating soil is much more common in plant-eating animals than in meat-eating animals.

Parrots gather at a mineral lick in the Amazon rain forest.

So, some plant-eating animals must also eat soil.

Mineral licks are places where the soil has many minerals. Some licks are rocks. Other licks are muddy or watery. At mineral licks, animals lick or eat the soil. They get the minerals they need. Animals may return to the same lick for many years. Many hooved animals go to licks. These animals include deer, elk, sheep, and goats. They will travel far to reach the minerals.

Fun Fact

Sometimes people put out human-made mineral licks. Then they can watch the animals that visit.

Over time, their hooves make trails to the licks.

Elephants visit licks to get salt. In Uganda, elephants also go into caves. They dig into the walls with their tusks. Then they eat the soil there. Elephants also sometimes eat the soil from termite mounds. The mounds have more minerals than the soil around them.

Even many kinds of butterflies eat soil. They gather together in one spot to suck up muddy

 Elephants dig into the soil for minerals.

soil. This action is called mud puddling. The butterflies need the salt in the soil. The salt is important for **reproduction**. The salt and other minerals in soil keep animals healthy.

FOCUS ON
Soil-Eating Animals

Write your answers on a separate piece of paper.

1. Write a sentence summarizing the main reasons animals eat soil.

2. Would you eat cleaned soil to treat an upset stomach? Why or why not?

3. Which animal eats soil for the salt in it?
   - **A.** elephants
   - **B.** dairy cows
   - **C.** earthworms

4. What would happen if there were no earthworms in the soil?
   - **A.** Plants would not grow as well.
   - **B.** The soil would turn to rock.
   - **C.** Plants would grow better.

5. What does **grinds** mean in this book?

*The grit breaks the food into smaller pieces. In this way, the grit acts like teeth. It **grinds** the food.*

    A. makes something into powder or little bits

    B. makes something taste better

    C. makes something have more minerals

6. What does **germs** mean in this book?

*They might eat food with **germs** in it. That can make their stomachs hurt. To feel better, the people eat clay.*

    A. small bits of food

    B. things that can cause sickness

    C. minerals that people need

Answer key on page 32.

Glossary

acidic
Full of strong chemicals that can break things down.

adapted
Changed over time to deal with a certain situation.

calcium
A mineral that helps build healthy bones and teeth.

digests
Breaks down food so it can be used by the body.

ecosystems
Communities of living things and how they interact with their surrounding environments.

minerals
Substances that form naturally under the ground.

mucus
A slimy substance found in the nose, stomach, and other body parts, which protects these body parts.

nutrients
Substances that living things need to stay strong and healthy.

reproduction
The way a living thing produces its young.

toxins
Harmful substances that are produced within plants or animals.

To Learn More

BOOKS

Duhig, Holly. *Garbage and Trash*. Minneapolis: Lerner Publications, 2020.

Mattern, Joanne. *Animal Appetites*. South Egremont, MA: Red Chair Press, 2020.

National Geographic Kids Almanac 2021. Washington, DC: National Geographic Kids, 2021.

NOTE TO EDUCATORS

Visit **www.focusreaders.com** to find lesson plans, activities, links, and other resources related to this title.

Index

B
bacteria, 5, 20
bats, 10
butterflies, 26–27

C
calcium, 23
chickens, 14
clay, 10, 12–13, 18–20

D
dairy cows, 12–13
diarrhea, 17–18

E
earthworms, 5–7
ecosystems, 6
elephants, 26

F
fungi, 12–13

M
minerals, 23–27
monkeys, 10, 18

N
nutrients, 6

R
rats, 13

S
salt, 26–27
scientists, 20
stomach mucus, 18–19

T
toxins, 9–11